THE *COLLECTOR* *OF* *BODIES*

THE *COLLECTOR* OF *BODIES*

Concern for Syria and the Middle East

Diane Glancy

RESOURCE *Publications* · Eugene, Oregon

THE COLLECTOR OF BODIES
Concern for Syria and the Middle East

Resource Publications
An Imprint of Wipf and Stock Publishers
199 W. 8th Ave., Suite 3
Eugene, OR 97401

www.wipfandstock.com

PAPERBACK ISBN: 978-1-5326-0300-6
HARDCOVER ISBN: 978-1-5326-0302-0
EBOOK ISBN: 978-1-5326-0301-3

Manufactured in the U.S.A.   OCTOBER 25, 2016

Contents

PART ONE

A Journey into Syria and Jordan

Our writing comes from forgetfulness, not from memory.
Ahmad Iskander Suleiman, Writer, Damascus, Syria

Hide me from the secret counsel . . . from the insurrection
[of those] who whet their tongue like a sword and bend
their bows to shoot their arrows—Psalm 64:2-3

Notebook of a Trip

Over a ten-day spring break, between the two wars of the two Bush administrations, I went to Syria and Jordan as an Arts America speaker for the United States Information Agency, when it was still in operation. I gave readings and lectured about Native American culture. I answered questions about America. They asked about the violence. Was I afraid to leave my house?

I remember stopping at the airport in Athens, Greece, where armed soldiers boarded the plane to search it. I remember landing in Cairo, taking off again, seeing a pyramid like a thimble on the barren land. I remember the square in Damascus where the driver pointed, that's where they hold public executions.

In Syria, I visited Aleppo University, the University of Damascus, Tishrin University in Lattakia, and Ba'th University in Homs, sometimes traveling a hundred miles between cities in an American Embassy van with a US cultural attaché, a visiting Fulbright fellow and the Syrian driver. In Jordan, I visited the Jordan Writer's Union, the Arab Writer's Union, Al Isra University in Amman, the Jordan University for Women, and various other groups.

Afterwards, the trip settled like an encampment on a hill. Maybe the trip was more intense because I was on land that connected to Christianity. The trip uncovered thoughts that had been pushed down by an academic setting. I heard, *we're people of the book—Jews, Christians, Muslims*, from the Muslims more than once. I was asked to explain Christianity—How it meant different things to different people. But for me, it meant salvation through faith in the death and resurrection of Christ.

Maybe the trip was more intense because Syria was the first time I was in a van stopped at check points by armed soldiers along the highway. Maybe it was because standing at the ruins of Ebla in Syria, there was an *older old* than any of the history I knew in America.

I wanted to *make use* of the disconnected sights jotted down during travel, the stops and intrusions, the interrupted fragments, the unrest of students in the universities I visited. *I don't want to be told what to believe*, they said. I heard their lack of possibility, their frustration, their anger.

I wanted to connect the Syria and Jordan trip to my other travels that semester, not always in chronological order. I wanted to work with the way memory works when there isn't time to order events. I wanted to convey the sense of hurry before I left—the papers to grade, a small roll-on bag to pack, a visiting writer who would not come to the door of the hotel when I picked her up the days and evenings before I left, but made me park and come in for her and wait.

What did I find on the USIA trip, but a glimpse of something I was a stranger to?—a subtle and diminutive shock wave, a silent yet definite detonation somewhere in the neighborhood—the clearing of smoke afterwards—the rubble. I wanted to record the quick look into a volatile place because it was all I was offered—and to leave with a sense that our words were something like tissue paper held over an open flame.

Damascus, March 24, 1994

There was darkness in landing. The streets inaccessible to light. The road from the airport—you didn't know what was there until you passed it. The walled palace in the city, a bedpost electricity had reached. The traffic circling at the foot of its hill. A voice from the palace saying, *if only we can keep them asleep.*

Down to the Simplest Wire in the Human Voice

1.

Once I was in a van in Syria.
The roads were like riding a camel.
There was desert cluttered with pebbles that seemed rubble,
but was standard for the houses in villages
made of stone and mortar

and next door the olive orchards and women picking there.
Or doing the work in fields where the country
was broken into with mountains and of course
the Mediterranean Sea.

By day, I traveled place to place,
making steady passage into the distance.
I took notes on the passing land—
a bump in the road, and the words I wrote
could not be read.
Or I made run-on statements of what I saw.
There is brightness of sunlight there is remoteness—
until I looked for meaning in my notes and found none
though I looked under the mountains and in the sea.

At night, the open windows. The dark sea by Jableh.
The waves of Arabic language rich with a new horizon.
I saw the eyes of people floating with curiosity
and mine at them as well.

2.

Every time I left a town I took the view of a boat
leaving the sea vacant there on the shore
as if the whole world were a broken slice of the moon
across the Mediterranean.

I tell you these valleys will run with blood
if these wars of nations continue—
these open, running sores
in the general way the world is moving
as if draining to a close

the way I shut my purse with a click
in the Damascus marketplace, the *suk,*
the burro with his dosser, the stalls of meat,
the home-spun silver pin I bought.

3.

Yet the road rippled as though a field
where an ancient farmer plowed his furrows,
and from my viewpoint,
when I saw more soldiers with their guns,
I knew no one in my country could tell me what
to believe
and I was happy about it.

Those beliefs have to come from within
or I would be at odds
as I was the day I went to the Muslim school for girls
and my heart sat a little at their desks, and the door
for me was in the leaving which they could not,
and among them were the people I met and spoke at.
They were kind you see and allowed me to talk
as the sun scrubbed the lovely sea at their port city
on the coast at Lattakia.

Wherever I went
the loudspeaker from a minaret read from the Koran
of the Islam religion into the streets.

What if they piped the Bible into my own country
on the corner of Market and Elm?

As I passed through Aleppo and Homs
on my way back to Damascus
I thought of the bylaws of my own country—
the triune system of Capitalism for greed,
Democracy for altruism,
the Judeo-Christian heritage for a moral component.
And the Syrian road where the apostle Paul was
dumbstruck[1] two thousand years ago
was brought right up front at last.

Something far away and remote
weighted its place in my bones.
Discontinuities or something like that
because of the conflicts and contradictions
in the human heart.

1. Acts 9:3-4

The University at Lattakia

> It's the writers, not the politicians,
> who should talk.
> A Syrian writer

A student in chador
had a question in the lecture hall.
The instructor tried to form her words.
I said, *let her speak.*
The tables climbed their ascending rows.
The windows scratched their throats.
She lifted a silent sky
from the bunker of our countries,
the Quonset huts of our eyes.

Can You Imagine Hearing No Stories?

1.

How do you begin a story?

You face the silence so dense the words are *magnetified* metal filings, but you begin to pry.

You put both feet on the floor you sit in a chair you open your mouth. You speak to the story as if it were already there. You remember a stray cat who came around and you left the door ajar and you saw him while you were at your desk from the corner of your eye he walked past the door one way then another and soon he jumped on your desk scaring you both but he was there and you reached out once and once again and soon he let you touch his head.

2.

No, you don't offer the story a corral or even the pasture.
You offer it the whole continent.

You hear a buzz, a hum, which is the clump that forms before a word.

You hear the word that comes from the hum.
Then others follow.
They stand together, shivering.

You separate the words from one another.
They won't want to at first though some come forward
to stand next to other words.
They learn to adapt, move over, and change in relation to others.

That's how story is a process of learning how to trust before you hear.

A phenomenon that nothing longs for something more than something longs for nothing.

3.

Your words travel the air-space between others, and there is a *hereness*, a connection, and soon your one voice is a cropduster that turns into a Concord when you see it's a matter of magnitude

say the prairie air-corridor at full amp.

Blue

The attaché walked me through the Damascus marketplace to a man—a dyer of cloth—who printed his patterns on cloth by hand—*buy one before he dies*—the attaché said—*before you leave this country for the next.* The man's shop was in an alley off the marketplace—there was an open door—the walls were something like adobe—there was a floor also of hard packed earth—dust—dirt—everywhere his jars, brushes, printing blocks, benches, tables barely standing—everywhere the blue the Syrian's love—the blue of their glassware—the blue of their desire. He sat wrapped in a tunic like the magician—the maker of patterns on cloth—something was said—he smiled—his discolored hands lifted to me blue and definite as words I could understand.

Despondency

There were times alone in my room, I felt the low point of travel. The weariness of understanding the fright of the world, or at least a variableness of it. So much larger than anything I had touched, but saw nonetheless, and could only express it sometimes in discordant images rolling against the other.

One afternoon I cried and had trouble stopping.

There was a muddle flying over the earth. A shard of fear. A distinct withdrawal from the awareness of the enormity of what was below and maybe above. What was the earth but a speeding story that maybe could not stop before it was too late for slowing? The unwrapping of other baggage I carried that would not stay packed.

This summit of one's self speaking before an assembly about the ordinariness of one's life because they thought all of America was rich. And to read one's work and have it interrupted by a professor telling his students the Arabic language was what poetry was, not the plainness of language I was bringing, and yes, yes, that was true, but poetry also carried the plainness of one's experienced life, and I continued my reading, and when it was over, the students shuffled by my table leaving mementoes and their thanks for what I brought.

Later in my room, I put my hand to my burning forehead, not with sickness, but with recognition of another part of the world. Maybe more than once I had the urge to fall on my knees and beg once more for what had passed.

Presentiment

The engines somewhere were running.
I could not hear them.
But I felt a vibration somewhere deep in the days ahead.
Sometimes when I woke
I felt we were already in the van
moving over the road to the next place on the itinerary—
a slab of unrest
making its way like a strong wind across the world.

Monday, March 28, Private Dinner Hosted by Bohemian Syrian Writers and Dissidents

I met a beautiful man who'd cooked chicken and rice and there was salad and other dishes on the table of his apartment. I hugged him when I left, held my head against his chest too long. We shared a kiss delicious as the meal, and he who said no English, said, stay with me. I couldn't, of course, you know regrets the next morning, the responsibility of responsible behavior, the diligent heart of a diligent nation.

But I would like to have, and felt brittle as my papers when they dried after I left them on the porch in the morning rain. He still holds me against him as if our ancestors long ago had left one behind when the other started out to reach a new land, because they loved the sea, because they loved travel, because they loved most of all the nomad of the human heart, or the camel-train starting out now toward the stars, because we're not satisfied, but striving down the ages to hold one another in that separation, that necessary departure, we're still having to leave.

Ebla, Syria

You stand in a country not your own. The ruins of the oldest city in Syria. The excavations opened in a country whose cravings you begin to understand. The sky as a whole toward whose reason the birds turn as a departure from this earth. How a people stay with you. How your attempts are a varmint in the way things work. Your tactics not solid as these digs, but you feel the blue glassware as you pack the plane that lifts it from the land.

Departure to Another Place

You change countries on a plane with Arabic writing. Your small roll-on luggage upright by your legs without safety regulations you know in your country. But a lunch that is right.

Sometimes I met in different places between classrooms and lunch rooms with students, each trying to say what they thought, what they wanted, asking if there was a way to take them. Later, the letters would arrive from young men with their photographs.

The trip felt like pieces from different puzzles mixed together with pieces missing from each. I picked up desperation. Maybe my own. I felt an insurrection, a rising of impossibilities wedged into hope, though the avenues were not there that would bypass the troubles.

It was freedom they wanted, a word so used in America its power was not as hallowed.

At night, in my room alone, I wanted to stay beside the awful hugeness of the world.

Bedouin Girl Reads about Transportation in Russia

1.

March 31st–April 2nd Jordan

On the road, the three-wheeled trucks overloaded
with people,
the hexagonal side-panels of metal,
silver, red, green,
like strange banners in a cathedral,
an ostrich feather on the grille.

2.

Above Amman, in the mountains, remote, windy, rainy,
a barefoot girl, a Bedouin, reads a schoolbook
the interpreter says is on Russian transportation.
If you told her how reading all that
she's behind the world's traffic
as she's ever been in your western thought.
She's reading wrong and out of date.
Their trucks would be your junkyard,
and you know how your country's arrogance
makes you smug and you unwrap it
like a tick as if it's simply uncontested.

The armed soldiers stand at checkpoints on the shore
where Russia peddles its hype to those who cannot know

the *jabals,*
wadis,
the windy villages, concrete-walled and cold-floored.

3.

You're a visitor to a country near the beginning of history.
You've entered the mess of influence competing
with interpretation.
You fear your own heart, and clear away
with your only hand the barefoot Bedouin girl in her village
you pass through wanting to say you're from a country
of transportation, but you know how seeing another country
makes you see your own
and you know how America's eye is always on itself.

4.

And when the Arab Writers' Union asks why America
favors Israel you say your country likes Democracy,
you say you're from a Judeo-Christian heritage,
Islam was not in your Bible except what departed
with Ishmael from Isaac,
you went to school with Jews,
they seem to have their place among decision-makers,
and your God, Yahweh, seems to be on their side.

5.

On your return to Amman you see the iron rods
the *hadid qudban* that stick up from the corners
of concrete buildings because it means
they plan to build more
and because they look like lodge poles in a teepee
having your land taken
the Palestinians relate to you
and you relate to the occupied territories
you see from the other side of the Dead Sea
like the Arabs' trucks dressed as gypsy tents
with green / red stripes and feathers for hood ornaments
their glories are in their going, their *yes* on the road
galloping between the hills as horses into a battle
they think they're destined to win.

Ding-y Bat Attackment

I dream just once in my life to hear a story the way the ancestors heard it. A full moon filling the land with its light.

Story the way it used to be making happen as the story was said.

The dark sky opened and you could see the condor in the hereafter where death was an arrest and everyone was seated by the archangels. A rowdy Mozart concert from the Middle Ages with everyone talking and eating. Babies crying and Beethoven was there wanting his turn. My own ancestors in the backstage, their voice *archivating* the hole and wholy mess.

Irrigation

I believe we're born in the darkness of the human heart
its landscape full of an alternating message not so subtle
saying, there is no hope but an intercessor who is the
waterwheel of my heart,
the *greater warm* saying,
we're caught in the bramble no matter how it is with us
if only in the cockpit we could see.

Histronics

1.

In the night, in the strange bed in a foreign land, I had a vision of a night sky with stars. The stars were yellow and they flicked like fireflies over a swamp in high summer.

I saw a black sky filled with stars. As if a dress sewn with electric elk teeth. They had a buzz of their own. Yellow *starz* they could be called.

I thought it was time to go to the afterlife. I waited. Maybe an elk would come to show me where to step off the earth into the sky I saw. My heart rumbled in my chest.

My rumba heart.

I thought the sky would come down over me like a teepee, the lining of which would be zipped with stars. Everything's gone modern. Even the stars move to some new source. *That's where we go, the ancestors say.* You know if you've ever had a front row seat somewhere, what it's like when you can see everything close up. That's where I thought I was. But I'd just woke from sleeping through a night. After about five hours anyway. Because I was in a time zone still off. But there was nowhere I could go without the guide, the driver, the embassy van. I thought I should just stay in bed, caught in a place I could not leave. But I had a companion that was the night sky filled with those yellow *starz*. Space is not space, but cluttered with bodies floating here and there as if your room was full of flyers and you had to duck or you'd hit your head on them.

2.

I thought of who I would see. Jesus, of course, and the Bible people I've wanted to see. They'd be off there in their desert tents in space, but I could stop. It was like sitting on Mount Nebo in Jordan and looking across the Dead Sea into Israel. *Something like Utah,* the woman said who drove me there. It wasn't a tour bus but a private trip. Like this one out to the stars. Close up, there are many more than we can see. Even more we can't see sparking like buffalo. But I wasn't a Plains Indian as they expected. I was from a woodland tribe originally from the southeast. The point from where the Cherokee people walked to Oklahoma before it was even that. Maybe the sky I saw was an early settlement. What the heavens looked like before it got to be heaven. When all the stars roamed like a herd we know was once on this continent.

And who else would I see? My father, of course, with his black eyes and hair. My mother. The relatives I knew. Mostly I want to see those I didn't know. My father's people who were gone before I got here. I tried to remember if I'd seen them on my way. I was coming about the time they left. Maybe we passed. You know those memories you don't know where they come from. The way you know a black sky filled with yellow elk teeth can move your dress even after you sew them on, and you wake in the morning and see the fleck-light you received in the darkness of this earth away from what matters to your heart, and you say *holy God* because you learned to pray according to the churches of your world. *It's where your home is,* your father told you, and lived away from it all his life, though he knew the sky was waiting. I remember when I knew he was leaving. Not that afternoon. No, it was several years later. But the vision of his death appeared.

3.

So now for a companion I have a night sky filled with stars. As if there was a sale on them. As if I was in surplus city where they'd been shelved from all the nights instead of in a foreign land—the militant buzz—the undercurrent of *Allah—Allah*—the power of something not mine—against mine.

Star City—I think of the avenue through which I'd walk to Christ the Christian religion taught. That we married God. No. We married Christ. He was the groom who waited for us at the end of life. Or who was coming again through the stars. Or sky. As if I was early at a wedding and had to sit there alone until the others arrived.

The stars were fireflies that attend. Or insects carrying candles or those pencil flashlights.

4.

You know each attempt to talk stubs the dark. But you open your mouth. The words will light their fingers as you talk.

You want to say about visions, they're true but maybe in a time to come. Or they're saying something now but you can't figure it out. Or in a certain combination of circumstances you'll know. Even though you feel you should be doing something in response to your vision if only you understood the sky at night. There were stars as if the sun had burst and filled the vast air of space with particles. They were thick as leaves you didn't want to rake, and have them all there facing you one afternoon when you decide you'd better rake your yard before it rains or snows and they pack like a concrete slab.

You try to remember if you'd seen that vision of stars before. You know when you were little and saw things on the ceiling of your room.

5.

While I listened for stories I did not hear my ears have fallen like dried mud puddles around my knees.

It's why I lift my knee to your mouth to hear your words. Tell me why the sky is black and pocked with yellow.

Tell me, Father, about Abraham in the desert hearing his children would be like the stars.

A Blueprint of Heroics

It rained the day we went to the mountains above the
Dead Sea in Jordan. The tents of the Bedouin women
woven from goat hair. The dog who grumped

because he had to move into the rain. We could have
stayed there at the edge of Mt. Nebo. The sun with
its steamers

across mountain roads. The dogs. Children. Women.
Chickens. The hot tea the oldest daughter brought
in glasses without handles. The children

rubbing us with their eyes. The smoke in the tent. The
skin full of goat milk. The dog returning. The Bedouin
woman

showing us how she weaves. Her first awkward step
across the floor-loom she straddles like a man riding a
burro no bigger than himself.

The Leaving

Long afterwards, I dreamed of being assigned a seat on the return trip. It was in a point somewhere inside the wing. I had to crawl through a narrow passage where I had to lie flat. I was held immovable for the 22-hour flight across the Atlantic.

In my dream, I had to find the way back, futile as determining wind-direction (at these altitudes) by a sock.

At the Poetry House, Tucson, April 27th

I want this yard to sink into me as rain. The wet fence, the birds over the porch where I stood in Jordan, the same walls pale as stucco, and windy as birds in the desert, their cries varying a rapid pace. The rain-spout clucking. You see an olive orchard when you can't remember which country you're in and what you've come to say. Or what words will come to you like a small animal looking at you from the desert floor testing your metal to be generous with your crumbs. The yard raked tenderly in rows and you think of the t.v. hooked to a car battery in the Bedouin village near Amman and you reach for the knob as if it were in your hand.

Jerney

Whoever can bear the discomfort of *inexactitudes*
and multiple complexities and contradictions
is meant for the kingdom

whoever can say that unity lies in differentiation—

the world picked up in a theater wide enough
to bear the whole of us up—

to see the multiplicity and not exclude
secures your part of the whole

the universe exists in particulars
and dividing lines

but how to mesh the different ways of seeing
when they are not compatible
when they always are changing and there's no *one* place

stories are a combination of all variables
with several ways of understanding—

a living coexistence of incompatible ideologies.

Near Tucson in the Desert

I will tell you how history inhabits every bone. How church was the roaster of our bread. How we prayed I remember at the altar between a beaten crucifix of tin and the heavy woodpews. The rooty bark of what they called yardtrees. Small and gangly. Your heart went jumbo because of prayer. The walls painted turquoise. A bowl of pins. A hose in the bare yard watering the openness. The voice of God was nothing more than the ground-fighters overhead. A desert basin clogged with roads to Antioch. Damascus. Leaves flying over the zone of every bird. The car alarm like a dog's yelp over the neighborhood as you neared the landing field of the mass. The sandy base of the yard.

Instructures

Heaven is hierarchical as the nights in the region
of the dream

you see blizzard snowdrifts on an instrument panel
fields disrobed

creeks dribbled by Jackson Pollack
if you get through the bureaucracy of saints

in the cockpit of their halos
the soft part of the temples where the horns

used to be
the taxidermy school

Preservation Avenue
and the crops

the economy moves faster
toward a one-world government

in the landscape of the presystem now
the underneath of surface abatement

all layers dowsed in the upbrush of the country
the dewclaws of animals.

North Dakota, March 4th

You hold on making a hand smoothing furrows
your fingers lined one beside another

your luggage stored over these treeclumps
a farmhouse maybe in them

the dining table of a sea
on which the continent formed with cold

the waves of your fingers trace snow
that lifts its breath across the window

you watch a blower clear the runway
as you bank over what is not your bucket of tea

a sound almost sky which spoons
a snag in the openness a knot in the fields.

Necessary Departures

You clunk your boot in the updust of religion.
There is no lightness here.

The forces rally in their own divided land.
It's hard to straddle the old argument:

Cain with the crops of his field,
Abel with the lamb

as he must have been instructed.
What floats inland as the only boat,

militant, avenging.
You see them in the shadows,

you hear them on the screen
grounding a different ground

than yours to stand on,
your indivisibility divided into units.

Not the justice you knew
when you heard the verdict

as we move toward the holy wars
at the headwaters of the world.

Moab

1.

At night, you hear the bells of goats climbing a narrow mountain trail. You wake and know it's vases on your fridge vibrating when they touch edges.

2.

You can't help but think of the old histories you passed in the Bible. The Syrian fields bleeding with wild poppies.

(If old Phoenician ships reached your continent, like they say, and not all Indians came across the Bering Strait, then they say you're related here.)

3.

You think of Islam as a code of ethics, a way of living on one's own strength. But you need an intercessor with might. You are broken. Supplanted. You walk foreign even among your own kind.

You feel a point of departure. You cannot co-exist.

If not the whole, a part to be withstood.

The Whole of What Story

For a moment there was air to talk of issues—to share the human fabric—in that brief space the U.S. spent its money to send writers to different countries—who talked of America—who said what it was before the military sent the whole of the story and how the softer words are shoveled under—and what missiles of language follow.

Roof

What do you do at the end of possibilities? When what you do isn't going as far as you need to go. When you've come back from a place that will not yet let you go. When you are under the roof that is too short for you to stand. You stoop in some way, your head against the ceiling. You find what will accommodate. You act as though you stand

because a roof is not a final place—
because it can be lifted
you find the loss and harness it
you say *move on*

there's an end of the trail you know you have it
the simple ordinary end of possibilities
as only the temporary limits to the house.

Tough Cookie

A myth means what can't be put a finger on.
It talks about something connected
but not directly with
because meaning is a dissembling of parts.
In other words the closer you get to meaning
the harder to talk about
because meaning is not a whole
but multi-placed as it speaks.

It moves to whatever dictates.

(As if there's a view behind a picket fence
the slats of which are staggered
so you can't see beyond
but as you walk
if you don't look directly
you can see the scene.)

2.

There's a story of a three-legged rabbit who made a wooden leg so he could
hop. This was during a time the sun was hotter than it is now, and the rabbit
decided to take a trip to the sun. The rabbit took his bow and arrow and
traveled where the sun lived. Each day it was hotter. The rabbit saw the only
thing that didn't burn was the cactus. He made a dug-out in the cacti along
the way, where he stayed during the day and traveled at night. When he
came to the east he saw the ground boiling and knew the sun was coming.

When the sun was halfway out of the earth, the rabbit raised his bow and
arrow. His first shot killed the sun.

3.

Now you think in terms of the (hic) too-hot sun.
The rabbit taking on the heat.
Showing us the unseeable in a way we cannot see
but looking to contingencies
and disseminating them
that's what myth does.
Otherwise (as I said) the sun would burn us up.

4.

Just look at the rabbit and the sun dispersing
until the myth's no longer the rabbit and sun
but their principles moving
which in this case:
imbalance is the Native American mode of empowerment.
When you're striving
instead of having achieved and sitting back
you can take on something in the neighborhood
of the sun.

5.

Which isn't the only point.

6.

A myth's a story moving to its separate parts.
Whatever situation can alter.

Meaning fits whatever can interpret
according to which is applied.

Get to the point the white man said
listening to the Indian
which is the point
meaning differently at different times
which dissolves our hope for a single melting pot
of simple outcome.

7.

At St. Lawrence Catholic School
there's a boys' door and a girls'.
Those words are cut into the stone above the doors.
I think that's how the rabbit lost a leg.

Pulling loose.
Or *trimming tulips*, the mind *knee-jerks*.

Think what it must have been traveling in the heat.
A prosthetic rabbit with a bow and arrow.
The possible *kulump* of the wooden leg
as he hopped.
The desert of the east
when the sun was living in the earth.
The lonesome journey where it boiled.

8.

There's also the aspect of myth as not true.
The connotation in other words.
The false leg. Or possible humility.

Oh there's no meaning here.
(All meaning does mean none.)

9.

But this hot is hot,
the rabbit thought as he traveled.
And took his pocketknife to the cactus
to carve a little house.
A picket fence.
After all he'd carved a wooden leg.
The walk maybe lined with jellybeans.
The roof sprinkled with paprika.
The kind of house you wanted as a child
when you built things on a summer afternoon
and found the earth thinning under the sun
and you could run anywhere
which is the meaning of myth.

Until someone had to *dosomething*.
Why not the rabbit?
It would be his arrow that killed the sun.

Having lost a leg
the rabbit could offer loss to others.
That's the principle of reciprocity
and he had the power of.

10.

Well, *giveit a chance,* the rabbit said.
The short-circuiting trip
between the variables of meaning.
The *scorched scene.*

Yes. Myth's a bag of jellybeans in a schoolyard.
A gist of all the implied.

The breadth of stars and moon.
The palpable dark of the heart.

A sun we still can't look directly at.

You Wild and Turbulent Riding a Big Machine

There was a band from Australia. Clapsticks, didgeridu, keyboard, guitars, microphones and microphones. They played *uhu uhu uuuh uuuuh*. Remote as the rocky roll just now finding their way through what'd already been done. You see I'm waiting for another band. The steam-clouds on stage. The flash of lights. I could hear the band of heaven ripping the sky. A young woman got up and danced in the aisle. Everyone looked. But this seemed something she had done before. Maybe an *oftengoer* to concerts. She felt comfortable as the blade of the evening. But all you can do here is run into the walls. And if you fly you have to come down. Hard. Flesh is limited to the *here*. But I want to go where the band splits space. Jesus, I can hear your drumming wheels. I want to line dance with you. I want to kiss the *starz* we pass.

Restorytive

The Holy Ghost to the human race:
How many sermons have you heard in church? The altar call to marry the
rest of your life. I tell you between the bars on the window of his kingdom,
the lead door, before it is too late, let his blood wash your heart, let him hold
open the ribs of your chest
let him lickyou clean all over.

Lake Winnipesaukee, New Hampshire

It was on a lake pure and clear he wanted me to join his life with mine and all the goops of history but I'd done it already I said and wanted loose from the trees to float over Gilford and Laconia the stars spread like heaven the next day the Bullockite Church—the barn adjoining the house—and all of New England against the piled-rock walls driving this whole place I wasn't from like a marriage.

Weaponry

The pink stemware on the glass shelves
  begins shaking.
      "In the Gypsy Settlement"
      Windows, Jay Meek

I was at a roadside cafe late in the dinner-hour when a car turned into the curb beside the booth where I sat. It was an old gray car with a windshield divided in the center—You may not be old enough to remember.

How spacious Oklahoma is. Much like the corner of Arkansas where we'd go when I was a girl. A car from the 40's not out of place.

We all know the mind exists trying to change the world according to what it sees, arguing with the best of them against the evidence contrariwise.

As you sit somewhere on the road, you know how you go one place after another until the succession of days flies like a stack of papers from a table.

It isn't the storms that invade the quiet your mind desires nor the circumstances that turn one over another much like the history of your driving after a tight semester you steer away from.

The Heroics of History

The immigrants to the northern plains
with their trunks and boxes
unloaded the sidewheel-paddleboat all day,
then took the sternwheeler upriver where it narrows.

A year later they come back.

You'd think the lesson was enough.
Winter abundant as the cold.

The only relief was the first burst of firelight
in the cabin.

The fields withstood them like an army.
The backbreaking effort of sod busting.

But the animals came to the edge of the clearing,
their religion intact
as they called to the God
who seemed only to answer back farther in the woods

from his sanctuary
where he knelt over his animals in the cold
rubbing their noses warming their toes.

Post Multiculturalism

1.

Crossing Kansas from the Rockies
is flat here too—the Middle East
except for rows of wheat, Interstate 70
and a few silos.
We started from a point of fog in the mountains
before dawn
where the *oneness of being* takes place,
when clouds come down and touch the trees
and animals.
It is stories that survive,
though the world works to stomp them out
as if fire hazards in a drought.
You remember the mufti
who called you back to his school
to tell the Indians of America to become Muslims—
to take the message to them.
But I know the crossing of the plains
on my own.
The mufti's one hand offered a message of peace,
the other,
a tarp for a dress,
a closure of thought.

2.

I could tell him when the last story is put out
the world goes with it—
It is something of what's happened in our lands.

He has a religion that is his state.
We have American occupation and manipulation
of foreign governments.

They asked how I could be critical of America
with an attaché sitting beside me
in the lecture hall.
Would I be hanged, beheaded?

I think of the inventiveness of our violence.
The sameness of each in different forms.

I think of the criticism
we have of our own country,
beloved as it is with its Walmarts and Wars.

Damascus Square

You would reach across the sea if you could
and into the land to touch
their rev of engines

the day in Damascus Square they closed
the schools and shops,
bussed everyone to show support

against American aggression.
You knew when you stood there
after the first invasion of the region

they were cornered from where you stood.
You see the square of television *satellited*
without translation. You know the divided voice

though it looks unified.
Their purpose of taking back their establishment
with motives for car bombs.

They see no other way.
They tromp the gas pedal. They will *insurge*.
They will rise.

You didn't know when you passed there
this land would haunt you,
this place that holds your hand.

Inviolate

> . . . the engine's afterburn, the tarmac's
> red glare . . . Red Able, *Falluja*

There in the alleys the boys learn war.
These are the lessons in the hot zones
when factions clash.
None quite right.
These forces in the hodgepodge.
These complications.
The war against the crushings.
These regimes of torture, hatred, fear.
The boys weep in dreams.
Girls too, who will mourn their death.
They are Noah building their desert hardboats
in the place that will pull the sea into it.

Pulp

I see the world as the history of a snake
tearing the earth for its nest.
The atlas of the world is news-print
left in the rain.
The snake twines through meridian fields and polar geographies
making cross currents in the world's traffic.
I see the earth as a drop-table desk,
the snake as front-yard grass.
I see the globe melting into camps.
The lawn of the world is open,
wires everywhere—

An End Note to Part One

By the late 1990's, when the United States Information Agency was folded into the State Department, Congress forced the cancellation of most cultural exchanges and the closing of American libraries and cultural centers worldwide. Then came 9/11 and the Iraq war and the abrupt realization that the United States needed soft power as well as military might.

"Rerun Our Cold War Cultural Diplomacy," Alan Riding,
The New York Times, October 27, 2005

PART TWO

The Civil War in Syria

The Watch

I return to Damascus—Galatians 1:17

I put my notebook in a drawer in the *afterbin*—the *after-having-been* in the Middle East. Once in a while I heard the eruptions of unrest on the evening news—or I watched a Charlie Rose interview with Bashar al Assad, the Syrian president, and felt the pages of that old notebook turn. Maybe it was the leaves I still had to rake from my yard. Or the wind across the plastic cover on a neighbor's boat at night.

I wore that journey like the tick bite on my foot where the small insect once burrowed into my skin and resided there briefly. But there was no match to burn out a memory. Not even the opening of a drawer one evening—the pulling out of words. I looked at them like the swollen place I found on my foot when I removed my sock, and wasn't sure what was there.

There was the visage of the trip I remembered. The receding relationship between a wad of news and some words in a drawer.

I went on the USIA trip with a commitment to the co-existence of differences. I flew on the hope for diversity. I returned with a departure from that. Not a departure from the people, but from the regime that held them in check. But what are regimes made of, after all, if not people who hold power over their own people?

When I watched the news of the political uprisings in Syria, I went over the words in my notebook, unfolding them from the trip I thought wouldn't last—just store them in the memory with dusty roads and mountains of a foreign land—the evening breeze off the Mediterranean—the students, much older now, caught in the upheaval in the streets of Damascus and Homs, Aleppo and Lattakia, who left their mark in my notebook like the tick's still-swollen mound on my foot.

The day we refuse to bow—3/18/11

4,000 dead
Syrian National Council
December, 2011

10,000 dead
Syrian National Council
May, 2012

20,000 dead
NBCNews.com
August, 2012

65,000 have fled
60,000 dead
January, 2013

Over 100,000 dead
August, 2013

130,000 dead
6.5 million displaced
2 million of them in refugee camps
hundreds of them dying of starvation
January, 2014

The Wind at the End of the World

It was near Detroit where I stopped to sleep
and later woke when a car pulled up.
Three men got out talking in their language,
laughing (quietly) as they talked.
It was the middle of the night.

Sometimes I travel after dark.
I stop at rest areas for a few hours to sleep.
I can lie down in the back of my car.
I cover a file box in the front seat
with a pillow and blanket
as though someone was sleeping there.

They wore baggy trousers.
One had a knee-length shirt over his trousers,
maybe tunic is the word
though the garment looks like a dress.
Kameez is a word I found online
when I looked up Taliban clothing.
The other two wore jackets
with their trousers tucked into their boots.

Over the years I kept driving farther and farther.
It didn't happen all at once.
Because I travel alone.
Because I'm no longer responsible for anyone.
I can drive 800 miles
dawn to dark, which takes longer to get to in summer.

The three men returned to their car and drove off.
My windows are darkened.
I have a way of hiding while I sleep
under the old paranoia
when Indians saw the cavalry
and talk persists to this day of poisoned reservation water
to get rid of them.
Get rid of them.

Twice I drove to the New England Young Writers' Conference
from Kansas to Middlebury in two days,
stopping for a night at a rest stop mid-Ohio,
and returned the same way.

Behind the world is a search engine
ferreting out its enemy
crossing borders
planning for its day.
They travel between their cells in our large cities.

One summer I drove from Kansas to Texas
to visit family.
From Texas, I drove to Head Smashed in Buffalo Jump
in Alberta
on my way to The Colony in Missoula.
I drove the 1,400 miles from northwest Montana
back to eastern Kansas in a day and a half.

They move at night.
I saw them when I stopped near Detroit.
How do I tell the dear ones of their coming?
How do I tell them we are nothing more than asleep?

Scorched Earth

A year later
the scorched earth is not drought
or brushfire
but a government's attack on its own cities
and people.
The opposition asks for guns to destroy the destroyers
but America already overstepped the world.
In Syria,
it's one Muslim group against another.
Meanwhile, a dead child passes,
laid in the back of an open truck
rocking over the gutted road
as if on an afternoon nap.

The Storm Wind Engulfing

A funeral meant for mourning turned to protest
against government forces.
A U.N. monitor truck destroyed.
Incompatible incongruities amuck.
A little trip to Syria
long ago—
people caught between Sunni and Shiite—
no room for those who wanted neither
but refugee camps now in Afghanistan.
To destroy everything
is in line—
a cruel regime and a Free Syria Army
shooting missiles to the sun.
It's like any disaster zone
that never strikes the whole place
but where it hits it hits—
I can still walk around parts of Damascus
a reporter remarks—
but Homs, especially—
in incoming blurbs across the bottom of the screen—
Iraq sending weapons
for the totality of chaos and war.

The Collector of Bodies in Houla

What is happening in the varied stories
and different versions that come?
Ever shifting but concrete in its shifting.
What can be trusted to be true
in the complexities of a country at war with itself?
There's a Syrian regime and a Free Syria Army
against that regime.
There are people in between.
But there's an outside force there too.
Artillery only government forces have
used in the massacre—
or it comes from the outside.
The Syrian government accuses terrorists
of giving weapons to the protestors.
Each has truth on its side.
The truth of the regime.
The truth of the Free Syria Army.
The truth of jihad and the moral code of Sharia.
The truth of the people on the street.
O cover that with your little words—
with their spider legs that crawl into crevices.
You hide in your own country with sympathy, yes—
but what does that do?
The children ravaged, women raped,
men burned in front of their families.
Outgunned. What can the people do?
What of the threaded versions that come into view?
Where exactly, the lines of embattlement?

O review it with your words one more time—
the divisions within—
then Iran, Russia, China, the Saudis—
the countries wanting their side of things
aiding the different factions of who knows who?
Then the Al-Qaeda forces that maybe come from the desert
or the Hezbollah in southern Lebanon
when all the people want is the freedom to buy and sell
and go about with their own little spiderings.

Now Homs Again

Now Aleppo and Lattakia
on the evening news
against a regime imploding like a dying star
taking the sky around it.
Wildfires in Colorado, New Mexico, California, Utah.
Possible hurricanes on the east coast.
The hostile politics under one's own feet.
You make a stance to hold the vents,
but the thought of meaning is involved.
How do you even think to say
how not involved is your involvement?—
the images on a flat-screen tv
at the table where you eat
watching war crimes
served with the meat and potatoes.

Pieces of the News (1)

A Cento for Syria

Syrian military and security forces assaulted Hama

Thousands of Syrians killed in massive military assault on cities ordered by Assad

eyes gouged, genitals mutilated, the marks of torture on the bodies of protestors returned to families—more evidence each day of what the state will do

We run a state system. We're enforcing the law.

10,000 hardcore al Qaeda-style jihadists have entered Syria. More arrive every day.

This week, Islamic radicals killed members of the Free Syria Army as they drove the rebels from the town.

The extremists carry out public floggings and executions.

Religion is everything to us.

Islamists hijack the revolt.

This is not what Syrians were hoping for when they spray painted *the people want to topple the regime* on city walls.

Iraqi troops abandoned Ramadi, leaving behind a number of artillery pieces, a half-dozen tanks, armored personnel carriers and Humvees.

If I knew two years ago what I know now, I wouldn't have supported the revolution.

A yearlong analysis of the FBI has concluded that controversial photographs showing the torture of Syrian political prisoners are authentic, providing powerful new evidence to support charges of extensive human rights violations by the regime of Syrian President Bashar al Assad . . . . The photographs, smuggled out of Syria by a defector two years ago, show no evidence of being manipulated and "appear to depict real people and events," the FBI concluded in a report compiled at the request of the State Department . . . . While the brutality of the Islamic state has been on ample display through its release of videos of beheadings, the far more extensive atrocities of the Assad regime have been less visible and have received much less public attention.

Syrian atrocity photos are real, FBI says.

Michael Isikoff
Chief Investigative Correspondent
July 14, 2015

Loading Zone for Interior Traffic

It escalates
uncovering a world
Biblical in proportion.
They fight with their faces aflame—Isaiah 13:8.
Their infants dashed to pieces—Isaiah 13:16.
Their eyes will not pity children—Isaiah 13:18.
It is written there—
whatever is found will be thrust through.
UN efforts against it have had no effect.
One bread store open—
Now hunger for the living in the rubble of demolished cities.
No delivery of mail.
No meetings or gathering of friends for coffee
in the sidewalk cafes.
There is blunt will and determination to destroy—
the houses full of howling creatures—Isaiah 13:21.

In a dream I climbed the stairs.

A white lynx with a row of horns along its back
and on its head
attached itself to me with its sharp claws.
A lurid glob of sound came from me—
a blood clot—
a cry of an animal taken down
that woke me.
But it was from my own throat.
Or was it them
crying out with their voices picked up in mine?
Do you know the rage of injustice?
This full-blown civil war
as yet without a finish or a name.
Not the struggle of the unions in my father's day.
Nor the killing of our own Civil War
my great-grandfathers fought.
They did not enter houses and kill women and children.
But in Syria, it is one brutal movement
against another.
The floors of houses streaked with blood
from dead bodies pulled across the concrete floor.
Blood spattered on walls—
puddled on door steps.
Soldiers shoot at those who flee to Turkey and Jordan
carrying their young across the border.
The families languish in crowded refugee camps.
What blazing place side-lit with sniper fire—
the rain, cold, poverty and hunger
sharp as the bite of a lynx?

The Cup He Cried For

80,000 dead March, 2013

In the newscast of upheaval—a two-year old boy stands
in the rubble of his house. He points to the wall nearly
torn from the room. He points to the disarray—jabbering
as toddlers jabber—making high-pitched observations
of what he doesn't understand. Then he sees his cup
on the floor. He points to it. He picks it up. It is broken.
He begins to wail.

There are feelings called upon to do what there would be
to do—but cannot. This dislodgment from everything
that is known. The crumbling of a child as both sides fight
to establish their brand of religion in a country breaking
its children.

What could be done to stop? To help? To say rest a moment
from torture. Or in your Christian view-point, you could say
there was a time when Stephen was stoned and looked up and
saw heaven.[1] You believe martyrs come back and drive up
and down the dirt roads picking up the dead. At night, they
fire-hose nightmares and bless the children in their dreams.
They stand with men when bullets rip into their bodies at
execution.

The newscast of the war in Syria barb-wires itself to your
chest. Look at the cup broken to hold the broken world.

---

1. Acts 7:55

Unknown No. 14

They can't identify the bodies of 20 children
wrapped in white sheets on the floor
like sidewalk chalk-marks that keep score in a game.

How does America face the dilemma?
Either way would be to lose—
unleash another war
or see the atrocity and do nothing.
The weapons of mass destruction in the last war haunt.

The regime should be stopped—
tried for crimes against humanity.
Yet is Assad holding back something worse
that would fill his place?

What if they are baiting America—
waiting for us to step into another morass?

A man holds up a month-old dead baby for the camera—
they call her Unknown No. 14
wrapped like a papoose from the Washita massacre[1]—
her face white from the poison they dropped.

1. Lt. Col. George Armstrong Custer and the 7th Cavalry attacked Black Kettle's camp
on the Washita River, 1868, Indian Territory, near the present-day Cheyenne, Oklahoma

Wired

A rebel builds Molotov cocktail-like incendiary
bombs in an abandoned school.
> *Makers of War*, Matthieu Aikins,
> photographs by Moises Saman,
> *Wired Monthly*, August, 2013

1.

The dreams I wake with
are residue of where I've been.
They are souvenirs from places I traveled.
This night I was in a house in the desert.
In the yard, a lion was eating a man. He said "help me"—
and I only wanted to go farther into the house
into a back room
where I could write about what I saw
and not be a part of what I knew.
Is nothing right with the human condition—
but should be uprooted, supplanted in its long history
of cruelty?
It is dreams that fork the council chambers and palaces
where plans are formed.

2.

I was reading a magazine when my car was getting new oil.
I was surrounded with signs for brakes, tires, exhaust pipes,
shocks, batteries, fender panels, fuel pumps, head lamps,
steering arms, barrel valves, engine mounts.
But in the magazine—a list of new words—

bomblets, mortar shell with twisted tail fins
as though a custom car.
Sacks of Turkish fertilizer, piping, bottles, liters, plastic
containers of all sizes for diesel fuel, aluminum powder,
napalm, ammonium, nails, steel tailings
to match a burning fuse or electrical spark.

An ammunition factory in an abandoned school—
cratered yard, pitted walls, broken window glass—
where the bomb-maker moves from lessons in elementary
bomb-making to antitank mines.

In the principal's desk, under a set of exam booklets,
a pressure-sensitive detonator.
Instead of a school bell, the sound of gunfire and
explosives.

I thought of the dyer of blue cloth in Damascus
on the USIA trip
in the clutter of the room.
What happened to the patterns and jars of blue?
The maker of them?

3.

A Google search tells you how to build a bomb.

4.

I suppose war becomes a way to see the world.

A civil war means a war within a country—
between them and not us—
yet they are hurting their own kind
as America was a hurter of its own kind
in the history of Indian wars.

But what to do as a leader of the world?
And what if the weapons America gives might be taken
by the wrong hands?
In the magazine article
there were pressure waves from another attack

from the regime.
Economic stagnation and isolation
and defiance of Assad.

"My dream is to go to a café with my friends,"
the bomb-maker says.

During the day, *a regime jet dropped a bomb*
burying three families under rubble.

And the photo of the people—
not looking at bins in the marketplace,
but searching for survivors after another rain of debris.

Prayer for Syria

> . . . the shepherd takes out of the mouth of the lion
> two legs or a piece of an ear . . . Amos 3:12

1.

The mountains of the southern California desert
look far away and docile.
They would not erupt.
Yet the ground is settled with dark soil and rock—
volcanic in their beginning.
Syria, when I was there,
was barren as the California desert.
Eruption was a possibility, even then.
I see long trains in the distance
like refugees streaming across the borders
of Turkey, Jordan, Lebanon, Afghanistan.

2.

In the mountains of Arizona there is rain.
East of Flagstaff, the odometer on my car
turns 200,000 miles. I wanted to see it when it did,
but was watching the rain that turned icy
in the higher altitude.

Two large trucks pass side by side
in the west-bound lanes
throwing trails of water behind them.

3.

Now in the darkness, the one bright light of a train
coming from the east passes in the desert of New Mexico.

Brush off your suit, Bashar al Assad—
adjust your neck-tie, polish your shoes.
You may be called to stand before the living God
with those bodies you've collected at your side.

ISIS

....and when, then, the imagination is transmogrified—
"Syria," Lawrence Joseph

... and mobilized with desperation and anger, a war-machine rises. I have
a friend who dreamed a snake crossed a river and became a dinosaur on the
other side. It is Terrorism, we agreed, returning to its primitive state. She, a
pastor's wife, I, a Christian believer, believe in dreams—or the interpreta-
tion of them. What else do we have in the wake of the awful happenings?
The children, reports say, are beheaded. Their heads placed on sticks. Is
it fabrication? Even Hitler did not do that—did he?—though we are now
in an age that has been *one-uped*. I have seen online photos—residents in
Syria who stayed behind when others fled, standing by the rubble of their
buildings. I printed out photos of refugees—a four-year-old boy found by
relief workers walking by himself in the desert. What is this Islamic Caliph-
ate? This worm in the center of the pistachio eating the core. It was sup-
posed to be a people's revolution cracking open an oppressive regime. But
it turned into fire. What is the heart after all? A brutality in the forest? No,
this is desert. What will they do to forgive the day? They are horrific, Chris-
tians said of Terrorists as they were air-lifted to France. Convert to Islam
or die. It was later that evening on television I heard a man—someone—a
US General—maybe—I didn't get his name—talking about ISIS. They will
know who they are up against if they come against us, he said. What was the
man thinking?—as if our resistance meant anything when planes flew into
buildings, and we entered a misguided war—or at least went to the wrong
place with our own war machines. The Terrorist gained force in the 2003
US invasion of Iraq. They took different shapes in the Syrian Civil War.
They continued to morph into more gruesome terrorists. Hyper-violent.
They murder dissidents. A pack of dogs that has tasted the kill. They have a
cause, a mission, a reason to be that gives them pacing. They want to be rid

of everything not them. Now the beheading of an American journalist apparently by a hand knife. Mark this day. They are moving. Maybe they will infiltrate unrest in various places. Maybe a natural disaster will demobilize an integral part of a country. Who knows? ISIS says the US is in their site. It is simple. A long dissatisfied history, not having a chance in the stakes. They will rise against American aggression. Even they don't know how it will be done as yet. Maybe 5000 killed in Syria each month. It is hard to tell. But there is unleashed fury. Last Sunday a girl maybe 6 was brought to children's church screaming, who continued to scream louder and louder. We could have prayed to remove the demon if we followed the possibilities of our faith. But it was more than we could handle. And backed off. Her father a tall, thin young man in a ponytail looked concerned, but someone talked to him and he left her there—and after church she sat in a corner playing blocks by herself—the storm stilled—for the moment anyway. Look at the ministers writing books—preparing sermons. As the days before the flood—ISIS is a direct threat, someone said on NPR during an interview. The US is behind on the ball. Trained fighters return home to cause havoc. They are a plane ticket away. They are crossing the border—former Governor Rick Perry said in Texas—you won't have to go to Syria. You will be able to fight them wherever you are.

The Loneliest Road[1]

Highway 50 across Utah and Nevada
something like the Australian outback
where I was years ago.
There is land and a road into the distance I follow.
There were spinifex bushes there,
and here, the small round clumps of sage brush
that blossom yellow in September.

I like to travel back roads
when I cross the country.
Anymore, my driving foot swells after two days
but I still can lift my foot to the dash
to rest my leg.
No one can see in this remote place.
I take my foot down if I pass a truck
or it passes me.

I listen to books on CD as I travel.
Now it is *The Yellow Birds* by Kevin Powers,
about his 2004-05 deployment to Iraq,[2]
which the wide valleys and stark mountains
also must resemble.

What I am struck with
is that the land also has seen war.
The upturned layers of rock in the little passes

1. A name given to Highway 50
2. A yellow bird with a yellow bill perched upon my window sill—the beginning of a US Army marching cadence

between the hills and small mountains.
The strata pointing up to the sky
after some old shiftings of the earth.
The buttes and broken gorges
weathered and lichened.
Yet the land remains.

Here it is the salt field of Sevier lake bed.
A basin that doesn't drain
but evaporates in the desert sun.

Between CDs, I hear reports on the news that ISIS
is entering the US across the border of Mexico.
If they can get past the drug cartels, I think,
who want the addicted in America to stay as they are.
There will be no swift killing of infidels for them.
They prefer a slower route.
I imagine new action comic books or video games.
The battle of ISIS against the Mexican cartels.

Maybe both will be endorheic salt pans
with no outlet but evaporation.

A few herds of cows graze the open range
with warning signs, cows on the road.
Not deer or antelope as elsewhere.
At various points,
the car makes a quick zipping sound
as it crosses cattle guards across the highway.

I travel for the assurance of the land
and its sorrow that rises
when one is alone for several days closed in a car.

I want to pass on a road whittled into the hills.
I want to cross this narrow ledge—
elevation 7,722 at Connor's Pass.
Beyond, the wide plain.
A heavy cloud.
The spit of rain.

Pieces of the News (2)

Several months ago, Wuhan University in China
posted a satellite image of the devastation
in Syria from the sky by showing the
expansive darkness over the country
at night. "Collapse of the Lights
in Syria." In Aleppo alone,
97% of the lights have
gone out.

As of February, 2015, 210,000 Syrians are dead,
verified by names, photos, documents, videos.
10,644 children and 6,783 women are
among them. 3.73 million have
fled, officially registered
as refugees.

220,000 dead
4 million fled
May, 2015

Until Nothing Is Left

I cut into an iceberg with an iron boat.
I am outside knocking on a door that won't open
and someone is coming with a fire bucket of coals
to place on my shoulder.
It is winter and the Manitou has ghostly breath.

There are stacks of pain on the wharf.
They can't see what is wrong
and I have no mouth to say.
There is fear in the unattended car.
What is that rattle in back?
Outside the window
sandflies.
The road jarred over a disrupted landscape.
A sweater of moth holes
as if my body shakes off and I am left without form
to blow away in the dismal world.

There is a formlessness without hands.
Start talking about something else
and the voice will be revealed.

Watching clouds is another kind of church.

I came to the place where thoughts stop
and there is nothing there.
A whirlwind delivered from the bowl
as if trying to speak while out of breath.

A refugee camp is a fleet of tents in the cold.
Leave a note—
There are holes in the sky.
Varnish peels.
I have to go through the sea
to find an iceberg for my iron boat.

Residue

A half million dead, March, 2016

Another morning I dreamed I was drowning.
It was easy to breathe under water
that entered the lungs with relief—
once the terror was past.
It was Bashar al Assad
who sent the flood of destruction
on his country
to maintain his kingdom
with an Old Testament edict
obey or perish.
He desecrated cities—
left his people tortured, dead,
fleeing to other places.
They are awake now.
The boats take them across the water—
overcrowded—overturning on the crossing.
Their bodies and baggage washed up on the shore.
They would not give up.
He would not let go.

Afterword

JULY 25, 2016, THERE was a headline on MSN.com—"Mysterious light streaks across California and Nevada." The photo of the comet-tail in the dark sky resembled wildfires at night burning in the west, as though the sky mimicked the earth, and returned the show. But it seemed to me a report of Syria's scattered fires from mortar shells and explosives still burning at night.

As a Christian, what can I do about the suffering in Syria? Actually, nothing— but pray and write about the concern. What do I think should be done? What according to conscience? To common sense? I could say invade, but the US has the lesson of Viet Nam.

Most of the men in my small family have served in war. My great-grandfathers in the Civil War. My only blood uncle in WWII. My only male cousin in Viet Nam. My only son in the Persian Gulf.

During a Memorial Day weekend service at our church, the choir sang *Battle Hymn of the Republic.* "He died to make us holy. Let us die to make men free." I could not hear the words without thinking of the importance of America as gate-keeper in the world that needs a keeper.

When I came across Jacob Hornberger's Blog online however— I saw the other side. He writes, "ISIS didn't exist before the 2003 U.S. invasion of Iraq. It was the invasion itself that ultimately gave rise to ISIS.

That's what sometimes happens when a foreign nation effects violent, involuntary regime change on another nation. The side that is ousted sometimes becomes angry and will do whatever necessary to regain political power. Recall the CIA's regime change in Guatemala which gave rise to a violent civil war that lasted for three decades, killing and injuring millions."

Meanwhile, I read in scripture— And when he had opened the fifth seal, I saw under the altar the souls of them that were slain for the word of God, and for the testimony they held: And they cried with a loud voice, saying, How long, O Lord, holy and true, dost thou not judge and avenge our blood on them that dwell on the earth? And white robes were given unto every one of them; and it was said unto them, that they should rest for a little season, until their fellow servants also and their brethren, that should be killed as they were, should be fulfilled— Revelation 6:9-11.

Maybe even the Lord himself stands aside until the time is fulfilled.

The story of Syria is the story of ongoing desolation carried in the arms of men, women and children in a country taken apart in front of the world.

It is the children, especially, who carry trauma to the next generations. For me, there is an image of the Boarding School experience for Native Americans embedded in Syria's civil war. There are the earlier massacres— Marias, Sand Creek, Washita, Wounded Knee, and all the lesser known ones. It is the upheaval that turns children into a rabbit in the heat of the sun.

Maybe Syria's effect on children is worse. Some of them, recruited by ISIS, have been taught to kill. They are promised help for their families, and a paradise for martyrs. They have seen atrocities we cannot image. Some of them have committed them. Other children sit on dirty mattresses in refugee-camp tents without school or hope of any kind of learning other than war. They can speak of a long list of family members who have been killed. Still others inside Syria climb the rubble of their houses with water and whatever supplies they can find. They live with the sounds of bombs, gun-fire, and the knowledge they could be hit at any time.

Meanwhile, the tangle of words from post-cities Syria—

Hospitals bombed. Airstrikes hit medical workers. Disrupted supplies of food and medicine. Munitions of chlorine gas. Disabled water plant and power plant. Collapsed buildings. Urban fighting. Violations of international law. Boy injured after Russian airstrike. Pulled from the rubble— blood running down his face. Parents and siblings also injured. Omran Dagneesh, 5. Beyond tears. Violation of international law repeated. Brother Ali dies. Human Rights Watch documents— a full folder of civilians withstanding an oppressive parent. The result of which is further oppression and fury. Incendiary munitions. Sarin gas. Artillery mortars. Barrel bombs dropped from helicopters. More children killed. Complicated oppositions— the tattered Syrian Democratic Forces for government opposition, al Assad and his government forces, Al-Queda, ISIS, local Arab groups, Kurdish militants and other off-chutes, Russian airstrikes, US special forces. Heavy military assault of banded weapons. Countries overflowing with refugees. We're in WWIII— King Abdullah of Jordan w/ Scott Pelley, ABC's 60 minutes 9/25/16. 160,000 Syrian children in Jordan's schools. We're in dire straits. ISIS only a small part of Muslims. Truce and cease-fire agreements interrupted. Iran 10/10/16— US attack against Assad regime would be suicide. Aleppo decimated.

How do you end a story that as yet has no end?

Damascus is taken away from being a city; and it shall be a ruinous heap—Isaiah 17:1.

As armies move toward Dabiq, a city in Syria the Muslims believe is a last battlefield.

Lord of mercy, have mercy on the changing uncertainty of suffering and threat as we are led toward peril by the pillars of smoke in Syria.

Acknowledgments

GRATEFULNESS TO THE UNITED States Information Agency for the trips to Syria and Jordan, and to Adam Ereli, U.S. Cultural Attaché, Samir Dahi, Syrian driver, and Allen Hibbard, Fulbright Fellow.

Blue Violin for "North Dakota, March 4th"

Burning Light for "Irrigation," "Roof," "You Wild and Turbulent Riding a Big Machine" and "The Heroics of History"

Caliban for "Instructures"

Colere (Coe College) for "The Cup He Cried For"

Duets, Handprint Press, University of Missouri, Kansas City for "Pulp." The poem is from a collaborative effort of visual artists and writers sponsored by the University of Missouri – Kansas City and Handprint Press. The project, *Duets*, was a random paring of visual artists and writers. I was placed with Larry Thomas, a digital print maker. I responded to his work because I resonated with the layers of meaning in *The Watch*. I wrote "Pulp" from his print. It seemed to sum up the intent of his work and mine as well. In his studio, I watched him manipulate the *transform tool* and the *wrap tool* on his computer to warp the words of "Pulp" into his digital print. The tolerance of the collaborative effort stood out in contrast to intolerance, one of the themes in which I was interested, especially as his print changed my poem more than my poem changed his print. The quandary continued as the evening news (especially the BBC) brought us the suffering of a people in a civil war— as we stood watching.

Five Fingers Review for "Ding-y Bat Attackment"

ACKNOWLEDGMENTS

Front Porch Journal (Texas State University, San Marcos) for "Part One: A Trip to Syria," "The Whole of What Story," "Despondency," "Ebla, Syria," "Presentiment," "The Leaving," "Part Two: The Watch," "The Storm Wind Engulfing," "Scorched Earth," "Now Homs Again," "The Collector of Bodies in Houla," "ISIS," "The Loneliest Road," and "Until Nothing is Left" (Texas State University, San Marcos)

Global City Review for "Blue" and "At the Poetry House in Tucson"

I-70 for "Histronics" and "Weaponry"

Image: a Journal of the Arts & Religion for "A Bedouin Girl Reads about Transportation in Russia" and "A Blueprint of Heroics"

Island Magazine, Australia Literary Journal, John Kinsella, editor, for "The Wind at the End of the World"

New Letters (University of Missouri, Kansas City) for "Prayer for Syria"

Quarter After Eight (Ohio State University) for "Down to the Simplest Wire in the Human Voice," "Damascus, March 24" and "Monday March 28, Private Dinner"

SAIL (Studies in American Indian Literature) for "Tough Cookie." The piece originally was presented as part of a lecture called, *Myth, Ritual, Desire and Cognitive Science*, University of Alabama, Huntsville

The Final Crusade: A Global Anthology, J.N. Reilly, editor, Glasgow, Scotland, for "Post Multiculturalism" and "Necessary Departures"

Widener Review for "Near Tucson in the Desert" and "Lake Winnipesaukee, New Hampshire"

Wild and Whirling Words, a Poetic Conversation, H.L. Hix, editor, Etruscan Press, for "Can You Imagine Hearing No Stories?"

Acknowledgment to the anthology, THE WORLD IS ONE PLACE: Native American Poets Visit the Middle East, edited by Diane Glancy and Linda Rodriquez, BkMk Press, University of Missouri, Kansas City, for "The Whole of What Story," "Down to the Simplest Wire in the Human Voice," "Histronics," "Necessary Departures," "A Bedouin Girl Reads about Transportation in Russia," "Monday, March 28, Private Dinner" and "Prayer for Syria"

ACKNOWLEDGMENTS

Acknowledgment also to the March 4, 2014 James Hedges Lecture, Azusa Pacific University, Azusa, California, for a reading of the manuscript, and the July 21, 2015 Thomas Zvi Wilson Reading Series, Oak Park Library, Overland Park, Kansas.

The Alan Riding's End Note to Part One used by permission of the author.

The words from Lawrence Joseph's "Syria," by permission of the author.

Jacob Hornberger's Blog passage by permission of Future of Freedom Foundation.

Michael Isikoff's passage by permission of the author.

The quotes from *Wired Monthly* by permission of the author, Matthiew Aikins

"Three-Legged Rabbit Fights the Sun" from AMERICAN INDIAN MYTHS AND LEGENDS by Richard Erdoes and Alfonso Ortiz, copyright @1984 by Richard Erdoes and Alfonso Ortiz. Used by permission of Pantheon Books, an imprint of the Knopf Doubleday Publishing Group, a division of Penguin Random House LLC. All rights reserved.

www.ingramcontent.com/pod-product-compliance
Lightning Source LLC
Chambersburg PA
CBHW071104090426
42737CB00013B/2471